797,885 Books
are available to read at

Forgotten Books

www.ForgottenBooks.com

Forgotten Books' App
Available for mobile, tablet & eReader

ISBN 978-0-243-47682-4
PIBN 10800857

This book is a reproduction of an important historical work. Forgotten Books uses state-of-the-art technology to digitally reconstruct the work, preserving the original format whilst repairing imperfections present in the aged copy. In rare cases, an imperfection in the original, such as a blemish or missing page, may be replicated in our edition. We do, however, repair the vast majority of imperfections successfully; any imperfections that remain are intentionally left to preserve the state of such historical works.

Forgotten Books is a registered trademark of FB &c Ltd.
Copyright © 2017 FB &c Ltd.
FB &c Ltd, Dalton House, 60 Windsor Avenue, London, SW19 2RR.
Company number 08720141. Registered in England and Wales.

For support please visit www.forgottenbooks.com

1 MONTH OF FREE READING

at

www.ForgottenBooks.com

By purchasing this book you are eligible for one month membership to ForgottenBooks.com, giving you unlimited access to our entire collection of over 700,000 titles via our web site and mobile apps.

To claim your free month visit: www.forgottenbooks.com/free800857

* Offer is valid for 45 days from date of purchase. Terms and conditions apply.

English
Français
Deutsche
Italiano
Español
Português

www.forgottenbooks.com

Mythology Photography **Fiction** Fishing Christianity **Art** Cooking Essays Buddhism Freemasonry Medicine **Biology** Music **Ancient Egypt** Evolution Carpentry Physics Dance Geology **Mathematics** Fitness Shakespeare **Folklore** Yoga Marketing **Confidence** Immortality Biographies Poetry **Psychology** Witchcraft Electronics Chemistry History **Law** Accounting **Philosophy** Anthropology Alchemy Drama Quantum Mechanics Atheism Sexual Health **Ancient History** **Entrepreneurship** Languages Sport Paleontology Needlework Islam **Metaphysics** Investment Archaeology Parenting Statistics Criminology **Motivational**

HOOLS FOR THE FEEBLEMINDED—THE STATE'S BEST INSURANCE POLICY

By IRA M. HARDY, M.D.

Superintendent of the North Carolina School for the Feeble Minded,

Kinston, N. C.

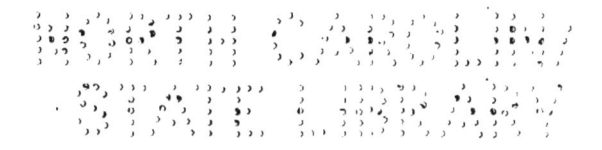

Reprinted from PEDIATRICS of December 1912

CHEMUNG PRINTING COMPANY
ELMIRA, N. Y.

SCHOOLS FOR THE FEEBLEMINDED—THE STATE'S BEST INSURANCE POLICY

By IRA M. HARDY, M.D.

Superintendent of the North Carolina School for the Feeble Minded.

Kinston, N. C.

In addressing you on the custodial care, humane treatment and scientific training of the feebleminded, and that specifically designed institutions for carrying out these laudable purposes are the best insurance policies in which the state can invest, I believe are such self-evident facts that they should need no other demonstration than that involved in the effective work which they perform for the unfortunate and irresponsible, and in the general uplift of society, and the wholesome regeneration which accrues through them to the state in the prevention and lessening of pauperism, degeneracy and crime.

Feeblemindedness is a very general and comprehensive term, applicable in a general way, to most of the shortcomings of private and public life, as illustrated in misgovernment of the state, the community and the family, and as exemplified in the diseased, the dependent, the degenerate, and the crimininal life of a very considerable portion of mankind. Taking the term in its broadest signification, it includes almost every phase of human life from simple aberrant mentality, through the various grades of neurasthenia, hysteria, epilepsey, and idiocy, up to clearly defined mania. All these various degrees of abnormality have their low, medium and high grades of development, with delicate pivotal balances alternating between under and upper normality, so that it is oftentimes difficult to distinguish the man or the woman who is sound mentally, from the unsound.

The tests which are made to determine the insane, established by alienists and scientific specialists, medical or otherwise, are of so searching and sweeping a character, that few so-called normal people could undergo the ordeal without in some degree being regarded as abnormal. However, we all know that the normalities of mankind far exceed their abnormalities, many of which have probably not so much to do with heredity, as with their acquirement after birth through accident, disease, isolation and environment. But to whatever cause due, we have feeblemindedness, with direct and indirect tendencies towards its alarming increase. It is not that it so much affects the individual and the family, but that it premates the community, the state, and the race. All these are so closely interwoven that what effects the one concerns the whole, whether for well or ill being.

Acording to my view of the subject, based on observation and experience, there are many degrees of feeblemindedness before idiocy or incipient insanity is reached, which could be either prevented, modified, or arrested altogether, before the opportunity is offered it to develop more serious and dangerous symptoms. From boyhood up, I have been more or less interested in such cases in my own and adjoining communities, and I feel and know that they had great influence on the trend which resulted in my adoption of the practice of medicine as a profession. I took up the study of the latter, not so much for its dignity and emoluments, as from the real desire to be of some benefit to man kind, and the number of years that I have practiced my profession has not only deepened and enlarged this bent, but has given me such an insight into the condition of the unfortunate, that whatever professional skill and manhood I may have within me, all seem to go out to the downtrodden, afflicted humanity, irrespective of any dollars and cents that may accrue from the work.

I have given earnest study to the mentally and physically deficient, and it has been done in a quiet and unobtrusive but nevertheless effective way—hoping ever, that if I could not, prevent, I could at least mitiagte some of the suffering in my midst and I have left to my brother physicians, who were probably more enimently fitted for the task, the care and treatment of the more general diseases of the public, while I more directly turred my modest endeavors toward the study and amelioration the mentally and physically defective, madeso either through inheritance, or by acquirement after birth. I felt that the well-born child, woman or man, in the exigencies of life to which they are susceptible, could be well and efficiently cared for by my professional brethern, while I had a different mission in life which I proposed to follow.

The result of all this, that in time, I was most fortunate to enlist the sympathy and co-operation of the good people of my state in this humane work, to the extent that through the legislative and executive departments, a school for the custodial care, humane treatment and scientific training of the feebleminded was chartered by the Legislature, and a state bond issue of $60,000 was authorized to begin the work. The good, generous people of my native city of Kinston, in the grand Old North State, made this laudable enterprise successful from the very start, by their munificent donation of nearly one thousand acres consisting of cultivated farm land, of pine and oak forests, situated within one of the most beautiful suburbs of the City, on an elevated plateau, gently descending to the waters of the historic Neuse River.

The state, in its preliminary undertaking, has now in the course of construction, rapidly nearing completion, the necessary buildings to care for—to start with—about 130 inamtes. These, in connection with the large farm and its appurtenances, will have nearly every needed requisite for their care and training, if not for their partial maintainence. As the superintendent of this inchoate institution, and as a physician, I appear before you to speak upon the great subject of the feeblemindedness of man, and especially, of that which pertains to the children, the woman, and the men of our beautiful Southland—to enlist your co-operation to the extent that your noble state, like my grand, old state, will take wise and prompt measures to prevent as well as to mitigate, the great evils which already accrue or may accrue from the feeblemindedness in your midst, so as to prevent its expression in pauperism, harlotry, or crime.

As yet, I come to you with no other experience in the line of institutional care of these unfortunate waifs of humanity, other than my observations, studies and researches in this particular domain of illy developed human life, with the added experience of years of medical practice and the careful observation of the workings and results acheived by institutions founded and operated for the specific purpose of preventing and assuaging the ills referred to.

Whether I am well or illy fitted to talk upon the subject of feeblemindedness, you must be the judge. I will say, however, that I am still the veriest student in this, the greatest of all the departments of sociology, and that it should take the precedence of anthropolgy, ethnology, and the other sciences relating to man and his subdivisions into races. It is the hand-maiden—the twin-sister of biology, as the latter applies to human life. I will endeavor, however, to give you my views, and why I believe, feel, and know, that the founding and operation of institutions specifically adapted to the care of the feebleminded unfortunates are the very best kind of insurance in which any civilized state or government can invest. In the first place, it goes to the very root of human life itself— to the foundation of every moral and law-abiding community—and lastly, to the prevention and mitigation of much of the human misery, pauperism, degeneracy, and crime with which the state has to deal. This has been and is being practically demonstrated by every civilized nation that has humanely and rationally taken hold of this great problem.

As I have already shown, the first step in the policy of the prevention and mitigation of dependency, degeneracy, and crime is to provide adequate institutions of the kind outlined, to receive the unfortunate persons who are so urgently in need of permanent care. And also, that if taken at the proper age, feebleminded children can be wonderfully improved. Indeed, it is said that if care for this class of feebleminded unfortunates were had adequately for a generation, the expenditures for prisons, reformatories, asylums, hospitals, alms-houses, police, and fire losses, would be enormously reduced, or what is even better, expenditures for such purposes would be accomplishing desirable tasks which we have as yet not had the courage undertake. The part the people and the state can take in conserving these human strains is hardly realized. We may say that the hereditarily defective child should never have been born, yet he cannot be put out of existence, but should be cared for, developed, and trained, at least, to the extent of being in a measure self-supporting harmless to society. In order to accomplish this with the least expense to the state, and with the best advantage to himself and to the community in which he resides, he should be taken charge of in his earlier years, which are the ones of his greatest receptivity.

Dr. Henry H. Goddard, who takes front rank among the highest authorities in the worl on feeblemindedness, and especially on the custodial care and training of such unfortunates, says: "It should be manual training first, last and all the time—training that is adapted to the child's special ability, making him happy, contented and useful."

This, I believe, will solve the problem of feeblemindedness, so far as it is capable of solution. We have now in America, as well as in Europe, large colonies where groups of these defectives live as nearly a normal life as it is possible for them to live. It is stated that they do the work on the farm, plant the crops, care for them, and gather them. In fact, they do all of the routine work of the old-fashioned farm, but always under the supervision and direction of expert farmers who are able to utilize their abilities to the greatest advatage. "They are perfectly content, and no one visits these institutions and studies the conditions, without feeling that here is the true solution of one of the greatest social problems that is now facing our advanced civilization."

To illustrate this more fully, I have before me the annual report for 1910, of Dr. Walter F. Fernald, superintendent of the Massachusetts School for the Feebleminded, at Waltham. This institution is a model one of the kind, and accommodates nearly 1,400 mentally and physically defective presons. As good work speaks for itself in the fact that the boys take livel interest and pleasure in the farm and the garden work. They do all the cultivating and harvesting—all the sowing and nearly all the hoeing. Other boys assist the baker, carpenter, blacksmith and engineer. The shoes of the nearly 1,400 inmates are kept in repair by the boys. The boys also do all the printing of stationary blanks, circulars, etc., for the school. They, furthermore, do much of the house work in the buildings where they live, and also serve as errand boys.

The girls are kept just as busy as the boys. In the laundry

they wash, iron and fold clothes. They do much of the darning, mending and sewing for the large household. Much of the children's clothing is made in the sewing-room by the girls. Every girl, at all bright, is expected to keep her clothing in repair. They are also taught to wash windows, polish floors, sweep, dust, and to make beds, etc. In the domestic science classes, the girls receive accurate instruction in ordinary house work—how to build a fire in the kitchen range, to brush the stove; to wash potatoes, to properly boil, fry, stew or bake them; to prepare other vegetables, to cook pork, beef and fish in the various ways; to make bread, biscuit and even cake; to lay a table, and to properly serve a meal. Some of the more advanced classes can cook an entire dinner. All this work is applied in the direct economy of the school. The pupils who do the best work in the classroom, are promoted to apply their acquired skill in the various kitchens and dining-rooms, to their great pride and satisfaction.

Some of the girls have developed a good deal of skill in cooking. Nearly all of them have ceased to regard kitchen work as drudgery. The older girls and women are of great assistance in the care of the feeble and helpless children. The instinctive love for children is relatively quite as marked with them as with normal women. A newly admitted child is eagerly adopted by some one. The affection and solicitude shown for "my baby" are often said to be quite touching.

This responsibility, it is claimed helps wonderfully in keeping the uneasy class of girls contented. Without this cheerfully given attention, the large number of children could not be well cared for without a considerable increase in the number of piad attendants.

The play grounds are equipped with swings, hammocks, tiltingboards, sand-gardens, croquet sets, etc., and each group of children spends part of every day in the playgrounds, aecompanied by an attendant who directs and assists in their games and sports. In the living-room of each group, is a liberal supply of bright-colored building-blocks, picture-books and playthings of every sort. Each little girl has a doll of her own, and e ch little boy, a sled, wagon or cart. These toys are always accessible, and the children are encouraged to use them as much as possible.

The playthings are not provided as luxuries, but as necessities if the instiution wants its defectives to approach the normal.

Indeed, it is said that to acquire alert minds, children must be alert. The young child can be alert only as his play-instinct is aroused. Shut out the play-instinct and you stunt the growth. Neglect to draw it out and you lessen the possibilities for strength. At least once a week, during the year, some evening entertainment is provided for the children, consisting of concerts, masquerade balls, minstrel shows, dramatic performances, stereoptican exhibitions, moving-picture shows, etc. These entertainments are gotten up by the officers and employees, usually assisted by some of the children. The moving-pictures especially, are greatly enjoyed by the children, and give them much real knowledge of the outside world. The most effective means of discipline, or sometimes for a misdemeanor or waywardness, is to send the child to bed while its fellows are enjoying one of these entertainments. This is more effective than corporeal punishment, which is not allowed. Each Sunday, services are held in the assembly hall, and consist of singing, Bible stories, simple illustrations and practical applications of the fundamental principles of morals and religion.

In the foregoing, I have endeavored to outline the most salient features of a properly constituted and conducted institution for the feebleminded, particularly as it relates to the care, treatment, and training of its inmates.

Turning attention to some of the general details in vogue in institutions designed for the feebleminded, I find that object-teaching in the broadest sense, is one of the prominent features of instruction. Objects, models, charts and other apparatus are employed for practical illustration. There are, however, other important features connected with such an institution in addition to its experienced and skilled medical officers and their specialized staff, including trained attendants and fieldworkers. Among these, is the school library for the teachers; especially one of standard publications on kindergarten and primary work, object-teaching, physical and manual training. There is also laboratory, dispensary, clinic, etc. It may be well to explain in this connection that field-work includes research of family stock, to record environment and parentage of the pupil admitted, or about to be admitted; also the number of feebleminded in the homes and at large, their condition, origin, and history back, at least, through several generations. This research work, in connection with the studies in the laboratory along approved lines of psychology, anthropology and clinical pathology, enable the institution to trace the individual defective from this stock origin, through his individual reactions, to institutional life in all its training features of mind and body, noting the modifying influence of such care and training on his growth and development.

According to the most experienced and skilled specalists on feeblemindedness—no one dares to say that there are no border land grades of mental defects that may not be conserved to the normal, if placed under an ideal life of training and treatment. This class is by no means small; but in addition, there is another class of defective children which should be g ven the benefit of the doubt—that backwardness does not always spell mental defect. To this "slight borderland—the twilight of the normal child mind—the trained pedagogue, psychologist, alienist and internist may well afford to devote their energies—not alone for the advantage of this group of backward children, but for the enormous flood of light such study will throw upon normal yet aberrant types of neurotic childhood."

To sum the matter up, institutions for the feebleminded, stand for the individualization of teaching and efforts at industrial and service training according to the scientific system evolved for the development of mental deficients. This system is over a hundred years old in Europe, and it is but in its infancy in the United States. However, the progress already made in this direction by some of the more advanced Northern and Western States of the Union, is unparalleled even in Europe. The whole question of the causes of feeblemindedness needs a thorough detailed study from all standpoints. Happily, now that state care and segregation of mental defectives is in the ascendancy of sociological progress, we may look forward to the ages to come when these ills will have been so well prevented that there will be no need for them or for dependent, custodial or penal institutions.

This leads me, to the consideration of the subject of marriage. Can it not be said here with truth that "fools rush in where angels fear to tread." There ought to be a uniform marriage law, intelligently enforced, which would be of great value in regard to the propagation of normal children. It is an acknowledged fact that law to be efficent must follow public sentiment, not precede it, and that which should relate to the uniformity of marriage should be determined by the broadest and most intelligent opinion in advance of the creation of a law governing the same. Fortunately, we are awakening to the need of perpetuating normal and healthy human strains. More than this, we are recognizing the possibility of still futher inproving these strains. The right to be well-born has been denied many. Society can redeem this injustice only in part, and for that reason, the very best that intelligence and science can give is imperative in concerting measures in the behalf of the ill-born. To the large and fortunate majority who have been well-born, education and a higher social conscience must not only teach real improvement, but also to use it in behalf of their less fortunate brothers and sisters.

Graham Taylor graphically expresses the importance of this religion of the future—the great sociological movement for the benefit of the race and country in general, when he says: "Religion and society, the church and the community, can not be separated. Reciprocity is more and more sought after. The church needs the social spirit and method of the best work of the community; and social work no less needs the spiritual ideals and sanctions which religious conciousness only can bring to any and every kind of service. The common ground upon which this religious conciousness in social work and the social conscioousness in religious work, are being born anew. In the process, work for the individual becomes no less indispensable, but all the more effective, and work for the community becomes less socialized for being more personal and human." Both religion and society are beginning to realize more fully than ever, that there is no greater danger to the neighborhood than the presence in it of mentally defective youth, ready at any time to indulge their uncontrolled impulses. And there is no burden that will bear more heavily on charitable or correctional institutions in the future, than that of the feebleminded offspring of feebleminded delinquents and dependents. But aside from the fact that as such grow older, and as the bad habits which they so early form become fastened on them, and the further fact that most of them are sure to have descendants even more feebleminded than themselves—there is also a very great danger of normal children being led into immoral habits by companions who are not mentally responsible for their acts, or for the indulgence of their uncontrolled impulses, which often lead to harlotry and crime. That such defectives ought to be early segregated so that they can not propogate their kind, nor prey upon the community at large, cannot be gainsaid. That segregation costs money is admitted, but that it saves money in the end if often forgotten. The initial cost of segregation or colonization is doubtless great, but the saving by counteracting our present lax methods would be far greater. As tax-bills are not itemized, the ordinary citizen does not realize that he is at present paying for the unrestrained presence of the feebleminded. An added tax for their segregation would be an apparant, rather than a real increase, for through the segregation of defectives, the number of criminals, the number of prisoners, the cost of court trials, the demand upon private and public charity, would be largely decreased.

Of the class of drunken sots, that make many of our problems in intemperance, a very large number of them are feebleminded. Aside from any natural or acquired mental and physical defects, it is a disease in itself, and never fastens itself permanently upon either man or woman, unless he or she has fallen below par comtally. If this abnormality were confined only to the victims emmselves, its effects would probably not be so lasting upon the hnemunity, but it has its visitations upon the unborn generations which make intemperance so abhorrent to all moral and right-thinking people. The same may also be remarked about prostitution, the largest per cent of the unfortunate victims of which, are girls and women of varying degrees of feeblemindedness. In this connection a prominent medical authority observes: "Let the public, young and old, be taught that seduction, one of the primary causes of the social evil—essentially in most instances, is due either to deplorable ignorance on the part of the man or feeblemindedness on the part of the maid. Its inevitable toll is physical and moral degeneration. It is fostered by mental and moral degeneracy, environment, starvation wages of feminine toilers, and extravagence. Let us come out in the open and fearlessly teach the plain people the plain home-truths about this largely preventable evil." Socially, let us put man on a level with woman, for where there is a fallen woman there is also a fallen man—yes, ten pure women to one pure man. The old saying that "an ounce of prevention is worth a pound of cure," is as true of preventing the ills to which human flesh is heir as it is of many other circumstances which concern human existence. Prevention is the best—but if that has not been used or has failed to be effective, then comes the next best thing to it, which is exemplified in the pithy adage of "A stitch in time saves nine."

Both these old adages are the quintessence of human philosophy and experience, and illustrate the best kind of insurance on the part of the individual, the community, and the state. This cannot well be gainsaid, for when practically carried out, it conserves human life and human affairs in the most effective form—improves morality, anchors Christianity more firmly, increases the general well-being, and saves the State the commission of needless wrongs, the people of much avoidable expense and thousands of heartaches.

Insurance of the nature and character that I have outlined, is the best of all, for it creates more demand for all other kinds. It represents no accident or loss account, but gain to all concerned. Its preminums are payable in manhood and womanhood regained, and its principal is invested in rehabilitated childhoodr placed on the plane of normality and health. No one unfamilia, with the subject, can estimate the incalculable good which such insurance will effect when used to found, to organize, and to operate specific institutions for the elevation of the misguided, unfortunate, degenerate, irresponsible, and helpless humanity.

Thus, it will be seen that the feebleminded instutution is the very best insurance in which the state can invest, for it deals with the under stratum of the social structure for its amelioration and generation, working it upward to a higher plane of existence and development, and lessens pauperism, degeneracy and crime. The latter are the great *bete-noir* of all well-regulated communities.

and give rise to endless perplexities in the government of states.

The desire of wise, right-thinking people the world over, is to better the conditions of human life—to uplift the mass of mankind—and not to force the weaker to the wall in order that the stronger may live. The latter are able to forge ahead and to maintain their allotted places in the body politic, while the former must have extraneous help, or they will continue to grovel in conditions worse than even death itself, for the latter puts an end to all their sufferings. If the duration of the influence on human life only concerned themselves, we might in the heartless language of conventionalism say: "Well and good, let them die and end it all!" But that is not the question, so much as the loss to humanity of so many of God's poor creatures, and the influence for evil which they may have upon the existing and coming generations of men and women.

The desire to elevate the average man and woman of the submerged stratum of society to a higher scale of progressive perfectness, is now being evidenced in Christanized communities more actively than in all the previous history of mankind. It does not rest in the good work for the fairly normal, but it seeks the debased adult, male or female, thus, pursuing hitherto untrodden channels of degeneracy and debauchery to their utmost lairs, whether it be in the home, in the dens of harlotry, on he streets, or in the institutions devoted to the care of the indigent, affliced, degenerate or criminal.

Some of these most commendable agencies in their remedial or reformatory measures, begin with the state—involving government, law, politics, morals, and society in their varied and extensive functions.

We, however, in our sociological work, believe in beginning with the child, and through it, reaching the parents and the home, and through the latter the various ramifications of the community, ultimately reaching he state, which is but simply an entity of the delegated powers of aggregated communities of the people. Sometimes forgetting its subserviency to the latter, in its various branches, it is the cause of many social and political ills from which the people needlessly suffer. Its poor-houses, reformatory institutions, asylums for the variously afflicted, penitentiaries and chain-gangs, get their recruits largely from the feebleminded. All these things taken together, with the crude, imperfect, and oftentimes corrupt legislation, and the strained technical interpretations of the law by our courts—have tended somewhat to the increase of pauperism, degeneracy and crime, rather than to their prevention or abatement. This, in conjunction with the many avoidable ills of childhood, motherhood and womanhood generally—have engrossed the minds, and aroused the sympathies of humanitarians and publicists everywhere to the extent of making sociological action imperative.

The latter is now being taken in a thousand and one directions but all verging to the one primal point—the uplift of downtrodden humanity. Is it any wonder than that we have suffragette societies, settlement workers, motherhood associations, children's aid societies, combinations for the prevention of the white-slave traffic and of the spread of the white-plague—betterment associations, Juvenile courts, and numberless other organized utilities for the care, control, and training of the helpless and irresponsible degenerate, not to speak of numberless other associations devoted to the regeneration of society itself, and to the improvement of popular government.

In all these sociological upheavels, or rather in the sociological progress being made on all sides and in all directions—none have been more marked of late than that which concerns the care, treatment, and training of the feebleminded.

As we all know, or at least ought to know, the latter as a class, have dull perception, feeble power of attention, weak willpower, uncertain memory, and defective judgment. I has been clearly demonstrated that to attempt to arouse these dormant faculties by forcing upon them the abstract truths of ready-made knowledge, is utterly futile. The teaching must be direct, simple, and practical. The feebleminded child must be made to do, to see, to touch, to observe, to remember, and to think. These faculties must be utilized to the fullest extent, and according to **authorative** opinion, the varied and attractive occupations and busy work which are so important a part of the modern graphic methods of education for normal children, must be utilized for sub-normal children.

This is only one part, although a most vital one, of the

great sociological work involved in the up-lifting of the child, the woman, and the man of abnormal characteristics, and through this means, forming the more perfect state, and the best form of government for the people. All these efforts, though radical and far-fetched as some of them may appear to unthinking eyes and ears--are nevertheless moveing toward the final good and betterment of human kind. They can never go backward, but must ever move onward—irrespective of illiterate conservation, untenable prejudice, illogical expediency, and the selfish interests of entrenched power for wrong-doing. All these things show that the world—that the common people who make it, and who do things, are trying to keep it moving along in fairly right channels. They are awakening more fully to the urgent demand for reformation, compensation and retribution, not only for the benefit of existing generations, but for those who are still unborn.

—Read before the Southern Medical Association at Jacksonville, Florida, on November 14, 1912.